SPORTS CAR
ORIGINS

BY MAE RESPICIO

CAPSTONE PRESS
a capstone imprint

Published by Spark, an imprint of Capstone
1710 Roe Crest Drive, North Mankato, Minnesota 56003
capstonepub.com

Library of Congress Cataloging-in-Publication Data
Names: Respicio, Mae, author.
Title: Sports car origins / by Mae Respicio.
Description: North Mankato, Minnesota : Capstone Press, an imprint of
Capstone, [2025] | Series: Powerful sports cars | Includes index. |
Audience: Ages 9 to 11 | Audience: Grades 4-6 | Summary: "*Zoom*! What is
that red streak going down the road? It's a fast sports car! People
everywhere love the speed and style of these sleek cars. But how did
they get their start? Who invented them, and when were they first
created? Discover the history behind some of the most popular sports
cars found on the road today"— Provided by publisher.
Identifiers: LCCN 2024004781 (print) | LCCN 2024004782 (ebook) | ISBN
9781669078869 (hardcover) | ISBN 9781669078814 (paperback) | ISBN
9781669078821 (pdf) | ISBN 9781669078838 (epub) | ISBN 9781669078845
(kindle edition)
Subjects: LCSH: Sports cars—Juvenile literature. | Automobiles,
Racing—Juvenile literature.
Classification: LCC TL236 .R465 2025 (print) | LCC TL236 (ebook) | DDC
629.222/1—dc23/eng/20240208
LC record available at https://lccn.loc.gov/2024004781
LC ebook record available at https://lccn.loc.gov/2024004782

Editor: Aaron Sautter; Designer: Elyse White; Media Researcher: Svetlana Zhurkin;
Production Specialist: Tori Abraham

Image Credits
Alamy: The History Collection, 13, The Picture Art Collection, 19; Dreamstime:
Imaengine, 27; Getty Images: Corbis, 22, Hulton Archive/Evening Standard,
7, Klemantaski Collection, 8, 10, 16, Popperfoto/Bob Thomas, 28, Topical Press
Agency/E. Bacon, 5; Newscom: Heritage Images/National Motor Museum, 26;
Shutterstock: Brandon Woyshnis, 4, Camerasandcoffee, 12, Felix Tchvertkin, cover
(bottom), ghiz, 17, Igor Krapivin, 1, 24, Lane V. Erickson, cover (top right), Mau47,
9, S.Candide, 11, Sport car hub, 29, SunflowerMomma, 15, Traveller70, 20, 23, Walter
Eric Sy, 25, WinWin artlab (design element), cover and throughout; SuperStock: Image
Asset Management, cover (top left)

Printed and bound in the USA. 5853

CONTENTS

Words in **bold** are in the glossary.

LIFE IN THE FAST LANE!

A sleek red sports car sits low to the ground. The driver hits the gas. *Zoom*! The car streaks down the road.

Ferrari 458 sports car

A sports car race in 1926

How did sports cars get their start? The first cars were built in the 1880s. They were slow. Some people wanted to go fast. By the 1920s, people began building fast and sporty race cars. Sports cars have some amazing **origin** stories.

FANTASTIC FERRARIS

Ferraris are fast! They got started in Italy. Enzo Ferrari loved cars. In 1908, Enzo went to a race. He was 10 years old. The race had lots of fast cars. Enzo was **inspired**. When Enzo grew up, he became a race car driver.

FACT

From 1920 to 1932, Enzo Ferrari raced on the Alfa Romeo team.

Enzo Ferrari in 1964

Ferrari 125 S car racing in 1947

Enzo later began to **develop** his own race
cars. In 1947, he built the first Ferrari. It was
called the Ferrari 125 S. It was fast! Its top speed
was 131 miles (211 kilometers) per hour.

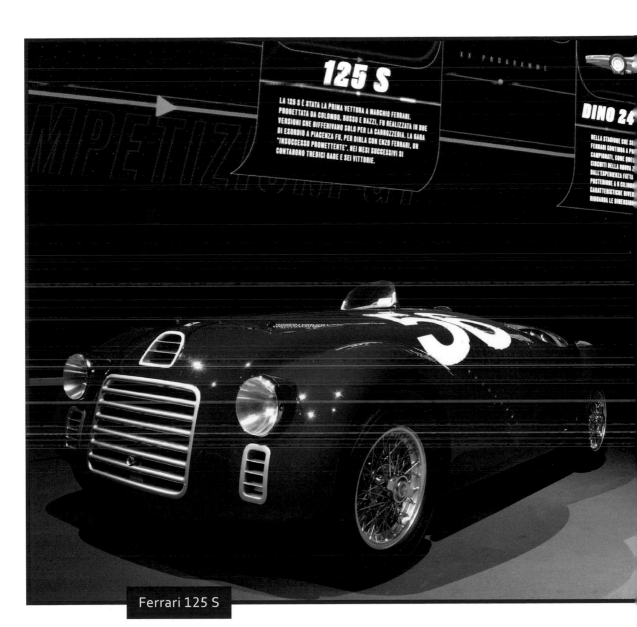

125 S

LA 125 S È STATA LA PRIMA VETTURA A MARCHIO FERRARI. PROGETTATA DA COLOMBO, BUSSO E BAZZI, FU REALIZZATA IN DUE VERSIONI CHE DIFFERIVANO SOLO PER LA CARROZZERIA. LA GARA DI ESORDIO A PIACENZA FU, PER DIRLA CON ENZO FERRARI, UN "INSUCCESSO PROMETTENTE". NEI MESI SUCCESSIVI SI CONTARONO TREDICI GARE E SEI VITTORIE.

XX PROGRAMME

DINO 24

NELLA STAGIONE CHE SE
FERRARI CONTINUA A PA
CAMPIONATI, COME QUEL
CIRCUITI DELLA NUOVA Z
DALL'ESPERIENZA FATTA
POSTERIORE A 6 CILINDRI
CARATTERISTICHE DIVER
RIGUARDA LE DIMENSIO

Ferrari 125 S

In 1948, racer Luigi Chinetti asked Enzo to make sports cars for regular roads. Together, they began selling Ferraris to the public.

Luigi Chinetti racing in 1948

Ferrari 375 America

In 1954, the first U.S. Ferrari dealership opened. The Ferrari name would soon be known far and wide.

LEGENDARY LAMBORGHINIS

Lamborghinis are **luxury** sports cars. Ferruccio Lamborghini began building them in Italy. As a boy, he loved helping his dad work on the family's tractors.

Lamborghini Huracán

Ferruccio Lamborghini with a Lamborghini car and tractor around 1970

When Ferruccio grew up, he started his own company. But he didn't build cars. What did he make? Tractors!

In the 1960s, Ferruccio changed focus. Why? He wanted a car that was better than another famous car. Which one? Ferrari.

Ferruccio loved cars. He had bought a Ferrari. But he didn't like the car's **clutch**. Sometimes it broke. He decided to make his own cars instead.

Ferruccio owned a Ferrari
250 GT Berlinetta.

Lamborghini 350 GTV in 1963

Ferruccio's car company was called
Automobili Lamborghini. It had skilled
engineers to design the cars.

The first **prototype** was the Lamborghini 350 GTV. It took only four months to build.

FACT

Police in Rome, Italy, use Lamborghinis as patrol cars.

The 350 GTV was introduced at a car show in 1963. But it had no engine! The car was built in a short time. The engine didn't fit. For the show, bricks were put under the hood.

Ferruccio (middle) with one of his engines in 1963

1965 Lamborghini 350 GT

Lamborghini **refined** his car's design. Then he added the engine. This was the first full model. It was called the Lamborghini 350 G I. It was released in 1965. People loved it. Lamborghinis have been popular ever since.

PORSCHE POWER

Ferdinand Porsche was an engineering genius. He loved cars from a young age. He had a dream. Ferdinand wanted to create a fantastic sports car.

Ferdinand Porsche (third from left) works on a car part with others in his factory.

In 1931, Ferdinand founded the Porsche car company in Germany. Did they build sports cars right away? No. They first made parts for other companies.

Porsche tractor

FACT

In the 1950s and 1960s, Porsche also designed and built tractors. Today, Porsche fans sometimes race these tractors!

Porsche 356

The first official Porsche model arrived in 1948. It was the Porsche 356. The car was a two-seat **roadster**. It had a rear engine. And it was super fast.

The Porsche 356 changed the sports car world. Its design set the stage for some of today's fastest cars. Today, Porsches are some of the best-selling sports cars around.

Porsche 911

MARVELOUS MASERATIS

In 1914, Alfieri, Ettore, and Ernesto Maserati started their own company. The Maserati brothers built their first car in 1926. It was called the Tipo 26. Later they built the Tipo V4. It was one of the fastest cars of the time. It could go 154 miles (248 km) per hour!

The winners of a class at the 1926 Targa Florio race in Italy drove a Maserati Tipo 26.

Maserati Tipo V4

Alfieri Maserati died in 1932. A younger brother, Bindo, then joined the company. The brothers kept building fast cars. Their cars won several major races, such as the Indianapolis 500.

Wilbur Shaw won the 1940 Indianapolis 500 driving a Maserati 8CTF.

Maserati MC20

In the 1940s, Maserati began selling sports cars to regular drivers. Over the years, Maseratis have become some of the most famous sports cars in the world.

FACT

In 1937, the Maseratis sold their company. But they stayed with the company to keep designing cars.

GLOSSARY

clutch (KLUHCH)—a device in a car used for shifting gears that is controlled by a pedal

develop (dih-VEL-uhp)—to create and improve the design of something

engineer (en-juh-NEER)—a person trained to use science and math to design and build machines

inspire (in-SPIRE)—to influence or encourage someone to do something

luxury (LUHK-shuh-ree)—something that is not needed but adds great ease and comfort

origin (OHR-ih-jihn)—the beginning or first stage of something

prototype (PROH-tuh-tipe)—the first model of something, made to test or improve its design

refine (ri-FINE)—to improve or perfect the design of something

roadster (ROHD-stuhr)—a car with an open body that seats two people and often has a removable top

READ MORE

Adamson, Thomas K. *Porsche Taycan.* Minneapolis: Bellwether Media, Inc., 2023.

Emminizer, Theresa. *Lamborghinis*. Buffalo, NY: Enslow Publishing, 2023.

Schuh, Mari. *Race Cars*. North Mankato, MN: Capstone, 2021.

INTERNET SITES

13+ Facts About Ferraris You Didn't Know
interestingengineering.com/lists/13-facts-about-ferraris-you-didnt-know

Ferdinand Porsche Facts for Kids
kids.kiddle.co/Ferdinand_Porsche

HowStuffWorks: Sports Car Information
auto.howstuffworks.com/sports-car-information-channel.htm

INDEX

ABOUT THE AUTHOR

Mae Respicio is a nonfiction writer and middle grade author. Her novel, *The House That Lou Built*, won an Asian Pacific American Libraries Association Honor Award and was an NPR Best Book. Mae has fun childhood memories of cruising around California with her dad in his 1968 classic Ford Mustang.